Plenty of Puppets to Make

Written by Robyn Supraner
and Lauren Supraner
Illustrated by Renzo Barto

Troll Associates

Library of Congress Cataloging in Publication Data

Supraner, Robyn.
    Plenty of puppets to make.

    SUMMARY: Instructions for making puppets from milk
cartons, cereal boxes, paper plates, egg cartons, and
other materials.
    1. Puppet making—Juvenile literature. [1. Puppet
making. 2. Handicraft] I. Supraner, Lauren, joint
author. II. Barto, Renzo. III. Title.
TT174.7.S96   745.592′24   80-23785
ISBN 0-89375-432-3
ISBN 0-89375-433-1 (pbk.)

CONTENTS

BEFORE YOU BEGIN:

Here are some hints to make your puppet making easier.

To make a square:

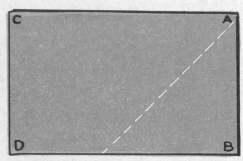

1 Fold any rectangle like this: Take hold of corner B, and lay edge AB along edge AC.

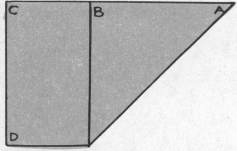

2 Fold along the dotted lines shown in step 1.

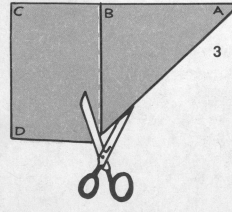

3 Cut along the dotted lines shown at left. When you open the paper, you will have a perfect square.

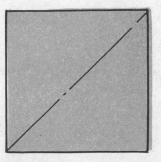

To make a cone:

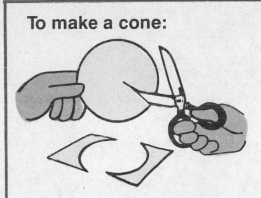

1 Start with a circle. Use a compass. If you have no compass, trace around a can, a coin, or a cup. Anything round will do.

2 Cut out the circle. Make a slit from the edge to the center. Overlap the cut edges, and glue them together. You will have a wide, flat cone. (*Note:* Bigger circles make bigger cones.)

3 For a taller cone, cut a pie-shaped wedge from the circle. The more you cut away, the taller and sharper your cone will be. Make a cone using only one-third of the circle. Do you see how tall and pointy it is?

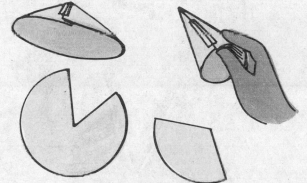

For putting things together:

Use paper clips, staples, tape, or glue. White glue, like Elmer's, is best for paper. *Be prepared*. Have everything assembled *before* you begin. If you are missing something, try using something else. You may come up with an even better idea!

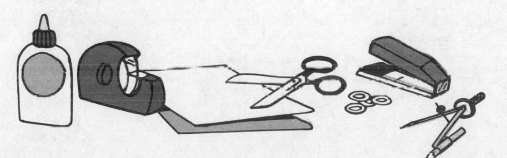

Use your puppets to tell a story. Use them to act out a play or a poem. Make them sing. Make them dance. Make them … and have fun!

INDEX CARD PUPPETS

Here's what you need:

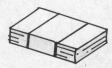

3 x 5 Index cards (Those without lines are best. You can buy them in white or colors.)

White paper

Colored felt-tipped markers or crayons

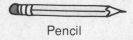

Pencil

Scissors

Glue

Here's what you do:

1   Grasp an index card at the center of its short sides. Use your thumb and middle finger.

2   Squeeze those fingers together and, at the same time, push against the card with your second finger. (*Note*: If you are having trouble, try making a small fold across the center of the card before you begin.)

3   This is your basic puppet. You can open and close its mouth by squeezing and releasing the card.

4   Make a snake or a dragon with a red, forked tongue and long, sharp fangs!

Draw the fangs and tongue on a sheet of white paper. Color the tongue red. Leave the fangs white. Cut them out and glue them in place. Draw snake eyes. Color them orange. Outline them in black. Cut them out and glue into place.

5   Color the inside of the index card red.

6   If you like, draw purple scales on the dragon. Glue shreds of yellow tissue paper under its tongue for flames! You can also make a girl puppet with long, curly eyelashes and hair. Cut and curl strips of paper for the hair and lashes. Use the edge of your scissors for curling. Glue them in place. Color the inside of the card red.

CEREAL BOX PUPPETS

Here's what you need:

Small (individual size) cereal box

Crayons

Glue or tape

Pencil

Scissors

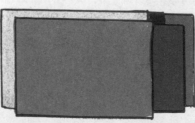

Colored construction paper

Loose-leaf reinforcements

Here's what you do:

1 Draw a line around the middle of the cereal box. The line should be across the front and two sides of the box. Carefully cut along this line.

2 Empty the cereal into a bowl, and eat it later.

3 Fold the box in half so there is a place for your fingers and thumb.

4 To decorate the puppet, lay the box flat on a piece of construction paper. Trace the outline of the box.

5 Cut along the outline, and glue or tape the paper to the box. This is the inside of the puppet's mouth.

6 Cover the other sides of the box.

7 Cut out a tongue, and glue it in the mouth.

8 Use loose-leaf reinforcements for the eyes. Sticky stars make good eyes, too.

9 Draw eyebrows and hair with a crayon.

On the next two pages are some other puppets you might like to make.

Use crayons to draw their faces. Cotton or yarn can be used for hair. Make a mustache. Make a beard. Add ears and whiskers for an animal puppet. Strands of yarn or pieces of straw make very nice whiskers. Use your imagination!

MILK CARTON PUPPETS

Here's what you need:

Empty, 1-pint milk carton for the goldfish

Empty, ½-pint milk carton for the frog

Colored construction paper

Scissors

Glue

Nickel

Ruler

Pencil

Black marker

Loose-leaf reinforcements

Tape

Here's what you do to make a frog puppet:

1 Rinse the empty ½-pint milk carton. Drain it, and pat it dry. This is your basic frog puppet. The open spout is its mouth. Hold the carton with your fingers on top and your thumb underneath. Move your thumb to make the mouth work.

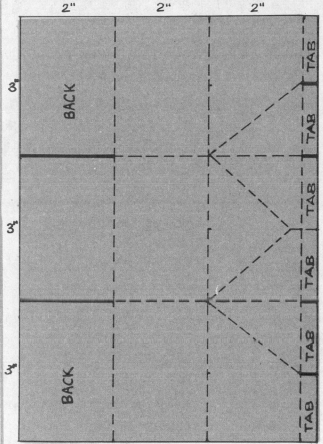

2 Cover the carton with green construction paper. Use the picture at left to make the paper covering

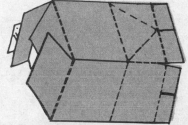

the right size. Cut along the heavy black lines.

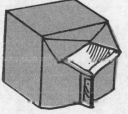

Tape the back tabs to the carton first.

Fold and tape all other tabs in place.

3 From black paper, cut out this shape. Stick two loose-leaf reinforcements in place for the frog's eyes. Fold the paper back along the dotted line and glue the eyes to the frog's face.

4 Draw two legs on each side of the frog's body, using a black marker. Glue some dark spots to the frog's body, too.

Here's what you do to make a goldfish puppet:

1 Use the 1-pint milk carton.

2 Fold a sheet of orange construction paper in half. Fold it in half again. And in half again. You will have a strip of paper that is folded into 8 sections.

3 Make 5 slits on each side of the folded paper. Make them about ¾" apart. Cut off the end piece.

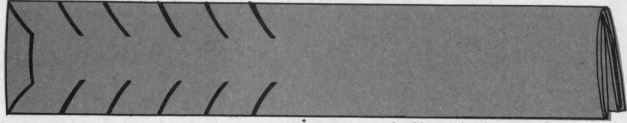

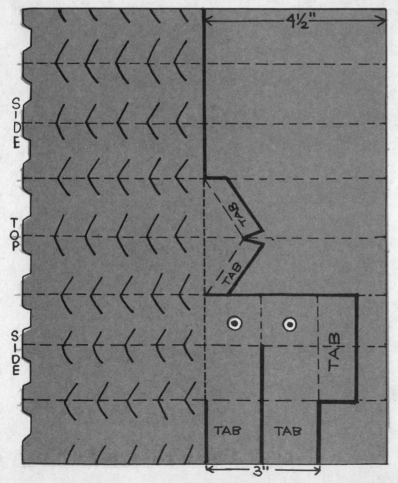

4 Now, slowly open the folded paper.

5 Cut away the part of the paper that lies to the right of the heavy black line so that just the tabs, the face area, and the body are left.

6 Draw 2 small circles on black paper by tracing around a nickel. Cut them out and paste in place for the eyes. Stick a loose-leaf reinforcement on each black circle.

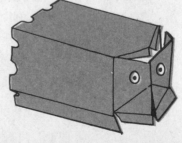

7 Gently fold the goldfish to fit the milk carton. Do not tape it yet.

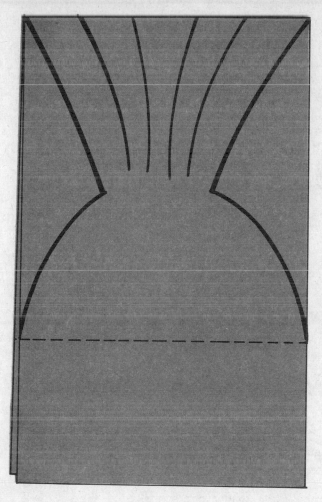

8 Fold another piece of orange construction paper in half and copy this shape on it. This will be the goldfish's tail. Cut it out and make slits in the tail. Fold both sides of the paper out along the dotted line.

9 Tape tail to the milk carton.

10 Tape the body of the goldfish around the carton. Your goldfish puppet is complete! Why not make a family of goldfish? Use a ½-pint carton for the baby goldfish.

PAPER PLATE PUPPETS

Here's what you need:

Paper plates

Colored pens, colored pencils, paints, or crayons

Scissors

Tape

Wooden dowels

Scraps of cloth, about 12 inches square

Pipe cleaners

Styrofoam balls

Tissue paper

Stick-on stars

Construction paper

Loose-leaf reinforcements

Scraps of felt

Glue

Sequins

Yarn

Buttons

Ribbon

Paint brush

Corks

Pencil

Here's what you do:

1   Take a paper plate and draw a face. Make it happy. Make it sad. Make it silly. Make it scary!

2   Decorate it with odds and ends. Use furry fabric or heavy yarn for mustaches and beards. They are good for making shaggy eyebrows, too.

Make curls by tightly winding thin strips of construction paper around a pencil. Add ears and whiskers for animals. Use corks for noses. Cut them in half or use them whole. Use buttons for eyes. These are only suggestions. Use your imagination!

Make a shaggy dog puppet:

1 Cut two slits where the ears will go.

2 Copying the pattern, cut out two floppy ears with tabs. Use construction paper or material. Brown, black, or spotted ears would look nice. Push the tabs through the slits and tape them to the back of the plate.

3 Draw two black eyes. Draw a circle around one of the eyes. Paste a round button into place for the nose. Add a happy mouth.

4 Cut out a long tongue and glue into place.

5 Cut lots of strips of yarn. Make different lengths. Glue the dog's fur to the face. Now your shaggy dog is ready to chase cats and bark!

Make a lion puppet:

1　Color the lion's face brown or yellow.

2　Glue yellow felt triangles around the lion's head and admire his mighty mane. Cut two ears and glue in place. Use a brown felt triangle for his nose.

3　Cut out two green triangles from construction paper. Draw black brows and eyes and glue to face.

4　At the bottom of the lion's nose, cut two curved lines and place an orange felt beard under the slits. Glue the beard to the back of the plate.

5　Poke two or three small holes under the lion's nose. Bend some pipe cleaners in half. Push the ends through the holes from the back of the face. Arrange the whiskers —fan them out. Your King of the Jungle is ready to roar!

Make a girl puppet with long braids:

1 Make the braids with heavy yarn. Tie them with ribbon, and glue them on. Use short lengths of yarn for her bangs.

2 Glue on paper stars for her eyes. Make a black dot in the center of each star.

3 Add rosy cheeks and a smile.

Make a clown puppet:

1 Use half of a Styrofoam ball for a nose.

2 Paste loose-leaf reinforcements in the centers of his eyes. Make them sparkle with sequins!

3 Make shaggy hair from uneven lengths of thick, bright yarn. Glue everything in place. Add a grin and crinkles to the corners of the eyes.

Here's what you do now:

1 For each of the puppets you'll need a wooden dowel and a cloth at least 12 inches square.

2 With scissors, make a tiny snip in the center of the cloth, just big enough for the stick to fit through.

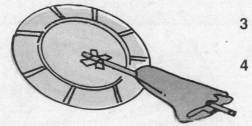

3 Tape the stick to the back of the plate.

4 The puppet's dress will hide your hand as you move your puppet about.

5 If you like, decorate the dress with some buttons and a pocket. How about adding a mouse to the lion?

EGG CARTON PUPPETS

Here's what you need:

Cardboard egg carton

Scissors

Construction paper

Loose-leaf reinforcements

Tape

Glue

Pencil

Black marker

Here's what you do:

From the egg carton, cut one of the tall crowns that separate the eggs.

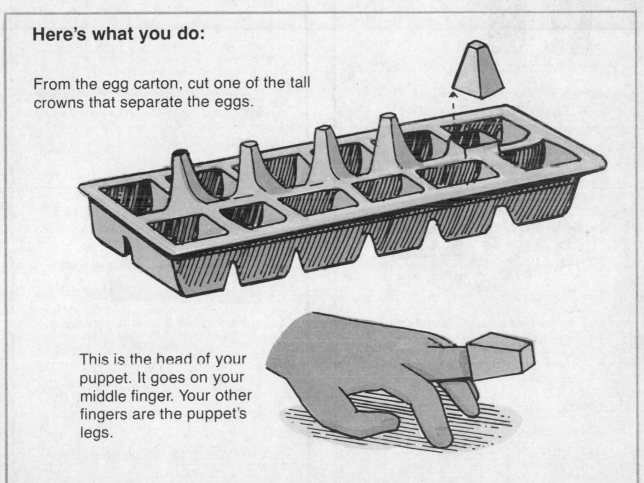

This is the head of your puppet. It goes on your middle finger. Your other fingers are the puppet's legs.

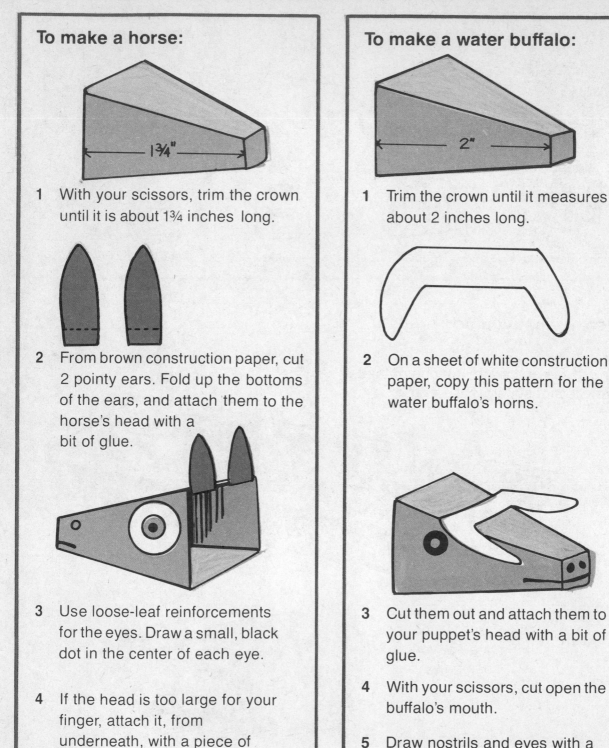

To make a horse:

1 With your scissors, trim the crown until it is about 1¾ inches long.

2 From brown construction paper, cut 2 pointy ears. Fold up the bottoms of the ears, and attach them to the horse's head with a bit of glue.

3 Use loose-leaf reinforcements for the eyes. Draw a small, black dot in the center of each eye.

4 If the head is too large for your finger, attach it, from underneath, with a piece of tape.

To make a water buffalo:

1 Trim the crown until it measures about 2 inches long.

2 On a sheet of white construction paper, copy this pattern for the water buffalo's horns.

3 Cut them out and attach them to your puppet's head with a bit of glue.

4 With your scissors, cut open the buffalo's mouth.

5 Draw nostrils and eyes with a black marker.

To make a giraffe:

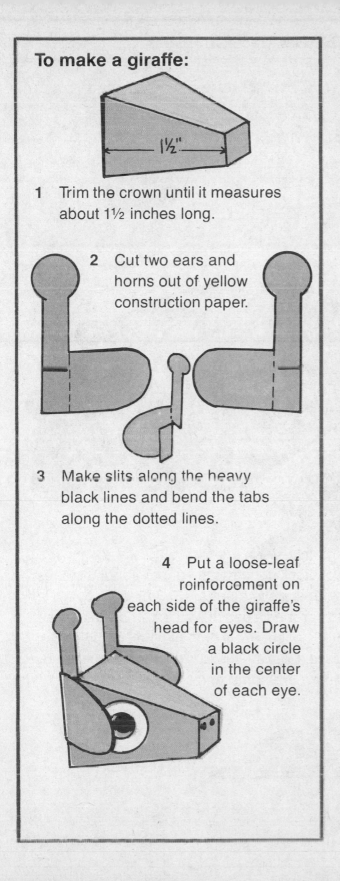

1 Trim the crown until it measures about 1½ inches long.

2 Cut two ears and horns out of yellow construction paper.

3 Make slits along the heavy black lines and bend the tabs along the dotted lines.

4 Put a loose-leaf reinforcement on each side of the giraffe's head for eyes. Draw a black circle in the center of each eye.

To make a wild boar:

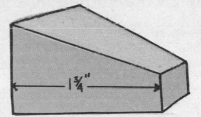

1 Trim the crown until it measures about 1¾ inches long.

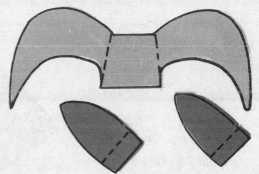

2 On a sheet of colored construction paper, copy the pattern for the boar's tusks and two ears. Cut them out and fold along the dotted lines.

3 With your scissors, make a deep cut in the boar's mouth. Slip the tusks in the boar's mouth and glue. Glue the ears in place.

4 Draw nostrils and eyes with black marker.

WALKING ANTEATER AND ELEPHANT PUPPETS

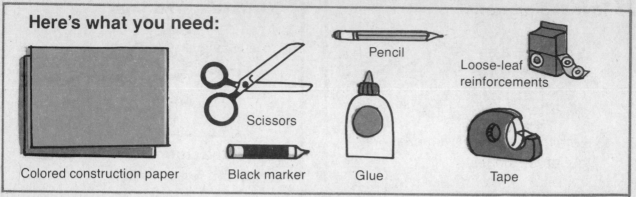

Here's what you need:

Pencil

Loose-leaf reinforcements

Colored construction paper

Scissors

Black marker

Glue

Tape

Here's what you do:

For the anteater—

1   Using the pattern shown, cut the shape of the anteater's head out of brown construction paper.

2   Draw two eyes with a black marker.

3   Roll the paper into a cone. Glue or tape it together. Bend up the ears.

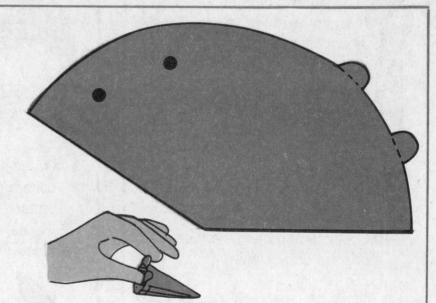

4   Cut a thin strip of black construction paper about 3 inches long. This is the anteater's tongue. Curl the strip by wrapping it tightly around a pencil. Make a small hole at the tip of the anteater's nose. Put a drop of glue on one end of the tongue and slip it into the mouth. Your anteater is ready —all you need now are some ants!

For the elephant—

1 On a sheet of construction paper, copy the pattern for the elephant's head or draw one of your own.

2 Cut out the head. Fold along dotted lines and tape together.

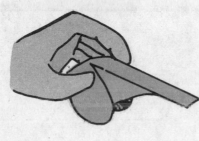

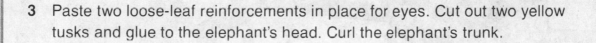

3 Paste two loose-leaf reinforcements in place for eyes. Cut out two yellow tusks and glue to the elephant's head. Curl the elephant's trunk.

4 Put the elephant's head on your middle finger. With your other fingers, take your elephant for a walk.

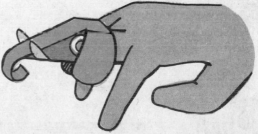

How about making a pink elephant?

DANCING PUPPETS

Here's what you need:

Crayons or felt-tipped markers

Scissors

Colored construction paper

Tape

Pencil

Shoe box

Here's what you do:

For the ballerina—

1   With a pencil, copy or trace the ballerina on a sheet of paper. Color the puppet with crayons or felt-tipped markers. Cut out two circles where your fingers will go. Then cut out the puppet shape.

2   Cut two rectangles of red paper. Make them about the size shown. Roll them into tubes to fit your fingers. Tape the edges together.

3   Put your two fingers into the holes from the back of the puppet. Slip a red stocking on each finger. Your ballerina is ready to dance. Just move your fingers.

If you like, draw a flower in her hair. Make a crown of sequins. Or cover her tutu with glue and sprinkle glitter over it.

For the ballerina's partner—

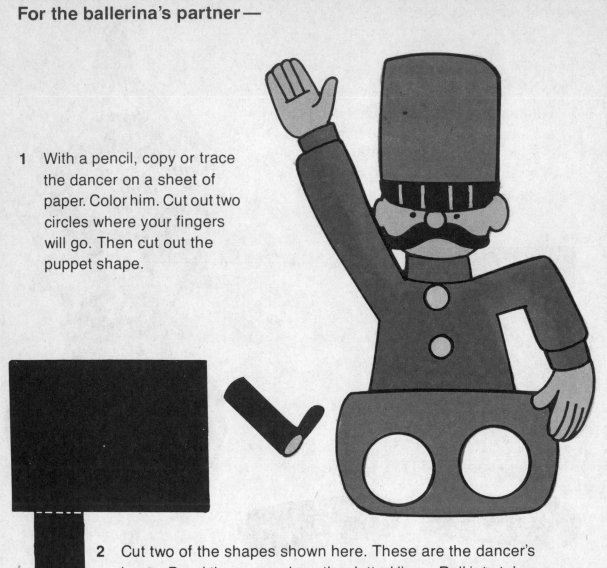

1 With a pencil, copy or trace the dancer on a sheet of paper. Color him. Cut out two circles where your fingers will go. Then cut out the puppet shape.

2 Cut two of the shapes shown here. These are the dancer's boots. Bend the paper along the dotted lines. Roll into tubes to fit your fingers snugly, and tape the edges together.

3 Put your two fingers into the holes from the back of the puppet. Slip a black boot on each finger. Now move your fingers up and down. See how high you can make him kick!

To make a stage for your dancers—

1 Cover a shoe box with colored paper. Use tan or brown paper for the floor. Add black lines for the floorboards.

2 Put different colored papers around the outside of the box. Decorate the stage with stars, sequins, or anything else you like.

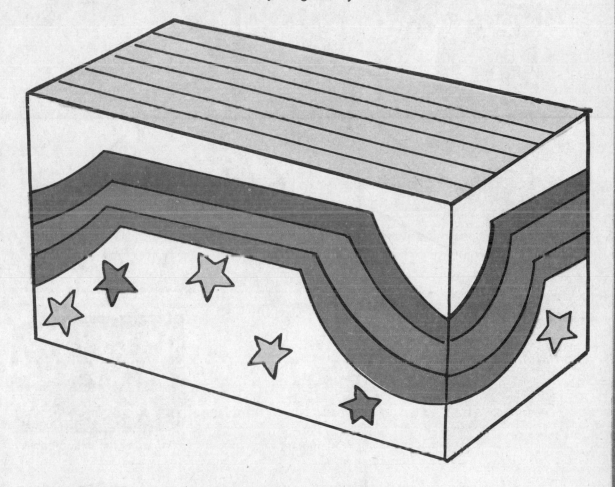

3 Play music or sing while your puppets put on a show.

CAT AND DOG PUPPETS

Here's what you need:

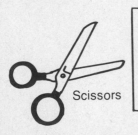

Glue

Crayons or felt-tipped markers

Colored construction paper

Scissors

White paper

Paper clips

Tape

Loose-leaf reinforcements

Here's what you do:

1 Fold a 9-inch square of colored construction paper into a triangle. Then fold again into a smaller triangle.

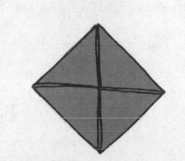

2 Open the sheet of paper. The center of the paper is where the folds cross.

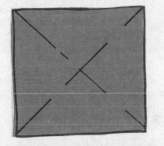 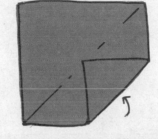

3 Fold each corner of the square into the center to form a smaller square.

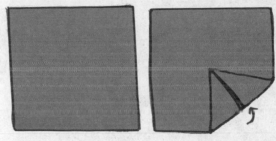 

4 Now turn the square over. Fold the corners to the center to make an even smaller square.

5 Fold this square in half, with the folded corners inside.

6 Turn the fold toward you. Grasp the inside of the puppet with your thumbs and index fingers and move the sides toward one another until they touch.

7 Put a paper clip at the top and bottom of the puppet to hold the sides together.

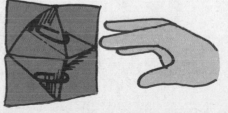

8 Slip your thumb and first three fingers into the four pockets. Tuck your pinky into your palm. You can work its mouth by moving your fingers.

For a cat puppet—

1 Draw green or yellow eyes on a sheet of white paper. Outline them in black and draw black pupils. Cut them out and glue into place.

2 Cut out a pink triangle for a nose and glue into place.

3 Cut a strip of pink paper for a tongue and glue or tape it to the inside of the cat's mouth.

4 Cut thin black strips of paper and glue to each side of the nose. These are the cat's whiskers.

5 Bend the tops of the ears forward. Trim the chin with scissors to make it round. Open your cat's mouth and say "Meoow!"

For a dog puppet—

1 Use a tan sheet of construction paper for the dog.

2 Stick two loose-leaf reinforcements in place for the eyes. With a black crayon or marker, black out the centers of the eyes.

3 Color the ears and a spot around one eye brown.

4 Cut out a black circle and glue in place for a nose.

5 Fold a piece of red construction paper to about the size shown. Fit it into the dog's mouth and glue into place.

6 Cut out a pink strip of paper for a tongue and glue or tape it inside the mouth.

7 Trim the bottom corners of the dog's head and bend the ears, one up and one forward. Your dog is ready to howl!

FINGERLINGS

A fingerling is a tiny puppet made with only a finger, a face, and a hat.

Here's what you need:

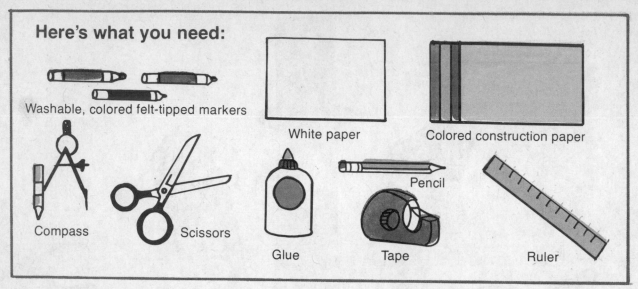

Washable, colored felt-tipped markers

White paper

Colored construction paper

Compass

Scissors

Glue

Pencil

Tape

Ruler

Here's what you do:

To make a witch's hat—

1 Use a compass to make a 1¾-inch-diameter circle on a piece of black paper.

2 Cut the circle in half. Use one half to make a small cone. Tape the edges of the cone together. This is the top of the hat. Make several ½-inch slits around the open end of the cone and fold these tabs up.

3 Cut out another circle at about the size shown. Cut out the center. Push the point of the cone through the circle and glue the tabs to the rim.

4 Place the hat on your finger. With a black marker, draw the witch's face on your finger tip.

To make a Foreign Legion hat—

1 Copy this pattern on white paper. With a black marker, make a black visor and hat line.

2 Cut out the hat. Roll into a tube and fasten with tape. Place hat on your finger. With black marker, add a face and monocle.

To make a French beret—

1 On a piece of colored construction paper, copy this circle. Cut it out. Trim it with a pompom, made by crumbling a small piece of paper. Glue the pompon to the center of the beret.

2 Roll a small piece of tape, sticky side out. Press it to the bottom of the beret and stick it to your finger. Add a face to your finger tip with black marker.

To make an Indian headdress—

1 Copy this pattern on a piece of white paper. Color it with your colored felt-tipped markers.

2 Roll it into a tube and tape it. With black marker, draw a face on your finger.

To make a mask and hat for the Masked Stranger—

1 Copy this pattern for the mask on black construction paper. Cut out the mask. Cut tiny holes for the eyes. Roll the mask around your finger and tape it.

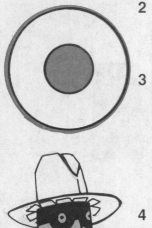

2 For the hat, cut a circle out of white paper. Make it about the size shown. Cut out the center of the circle.

3 Cut a rectangle of white paper as shown. Roll it into a tube to fit into the inner circle of the hat's brim. Tape the edges of the tube together. Make several ⅛-inch slits around one edge of the tube and fold these flaps up.

4 Snip off the opposite sides of the top of the hat. Place cone in brim and glue flaps to brim. Put hat on finger and add the face.

To make a hat for Robin Hood—

1 Cut a piece of green construction paper about this size. Fold in half along dotted lines. Then fold over two flaps to make a triangle. Fold the two bottom flaps up.

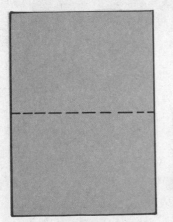

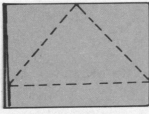

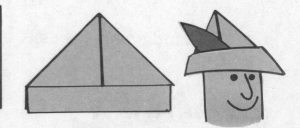

2 Fold all four tips into the hat. Cut out a small red feather and glue to hat. Place the hat on your finger and add Robin's face.

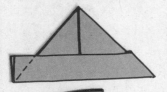

To make a Mexican sombrero—

1 Copy this pattern on yellow construction paper. Cut it out. Decorate the brim and then curl it slightly.

2 Cut another piece of yellow paper in this shape. Roll it into a cone to fit into the brim. Tape the edges together. Make several slits around the open end of the cone and fold up these flaps. Put the cone into the brim and glue flaps to brim.

3 Put the sombrero on your finger and add a face.

To make Abe Lincoln's top hat—

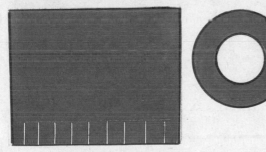

1 Cut these two shapes out of black or dark blue construction paper. Roll the rectangle into a tube that will fit into the hole of the other shape. Tape the edges of the tube together. Make several 1/8-inch slits around one edge of the tube and fold up these flaps. Put tube into the brim and glue flaps to it.

2 Place hat on your finger. With black marker, add nose, mouth, and beard.

You can create a professor by making eyeglasses to tape around your finger. Use cotton for his hair.

The swami wears a turban. Use a thin strip of white paper. Wrap it around your finger and tape it. Draw the swami's face.

Now your Fingerlings are ready for action. Tell a story and let your fingers act it out.

GEORGE AND GUSSIE GOOSE

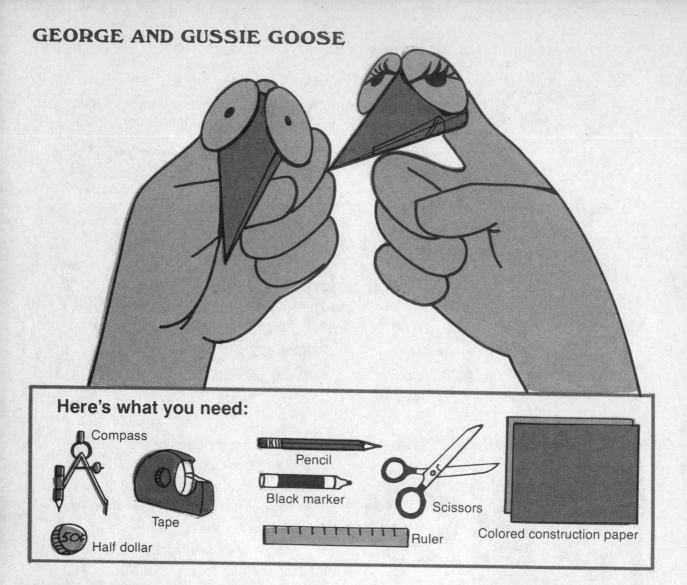

Here's what you need:

Compass

Tape

Half dollar

Pencil

Black marker

Scissors

Ruler

Colored construction paper

Here's what you do:

1 Set the compass at 2¾ inches and draw a
circle on orange construction paper. The circle
will measure 5½ inches across. (If you don't
have a compass, trace around a coffee can or a
small saucer.) Cut out the circle.

2 Using the half dollar, trace four circles on a piece of yellow construction paper. Outline each one with black marker and draw a black spot in the center of each. These are George's and Gussie's eyes. Cut them out.

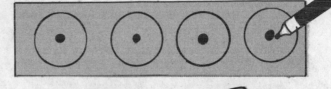

3 Take the large orange circle and cut it in half. Fold each half in half.

4 Roll each folded half into a cone. Tape the edges together. These are the beaks.

5 Roll a small piece of tape with the sticky side out. Press it to the back of an eye and stick it in place on the beak. Repeat for the other eye. This is George.

6 For Gussie, do the same. You may want to add eyelashes to her eyes.

7 Slip each of your index fingers into a puppet.

PIRATE PUPPETS AND STAGE

Here's what you need:

Black marker

Pieces of colored felt

Tape

Scissors

Colored construction paper

Corrugated cardboard box

Here's what you do:

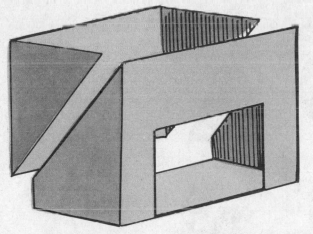

For the stage—

1 Cut the cardboard box as shown. The part with the rectangular opening is the stage.

2 Cut a long strip from the remaining part of the box. Bend it as shown below.

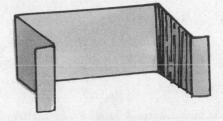

3 Glue the strip to the stage.

4 Decorate the front of the stage any way you like. Put stars, colors, or a banner on it. Use your imagination!

5 Place the stage on a table so you can stand behind it and give a puppet show.

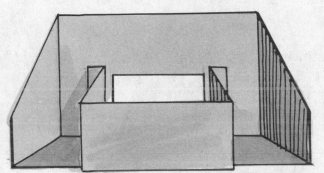

For the pirates—

(Note that you may need the help of a friend to draw the faces on your hands.)

1 For the first pirate, wrap a piece of felt or cloth around your hand and knot it.

2 Cut out a black patch and tape it in place.

3 Wrap a piece of felt around your first and second fingers and tape the ends together.

4 With a black marker, draw an eye, mouth, nose, and beard.

1 For the pirate captain, cut a large circle out of dark blue or black construction paper. Make an opening in the middle of the paper to put your hand through. Bend up both sides of the captain's hat.

2 Cut out a skull and crossbones and glue it to hat.

3 Wrap a piece of felt around your fingers as shown.

4 Draw eyes, nose, and mustache with black marker. Now your pirates are ready to hop aboard their stage!